The Bumper Book of Silly Short Jokes and One-Liners

Volume One

Ted Martins

Contents

Introduction

This book has a large range of hilarious one liners, puns and other groaners that will give you lots of laughter – or hopefully at least one laugh!

There are jokes on a wide range of topics. Hopefully there will be many jokes you have not heard before.

Cheer yourself up with this bumper book of carefully selected hilarious and silly jokes!

The Jokes

My foot was run over by a rental car. It Hertz.

-

I grew up in a poor part of town in Italy - a spaghetto.

-

The police are looking for a man with one eye. They could not find him using two eyes so thought this would help.

-

My bicycle fell over. It was too tired.

-

A tramp slept on old magazines. He had lots of back issues.

-

How do you make a pirate angry. Take the P out of him.

-

I name people I meet after shops. You are Next.

What are the species of Bees called that live in America? USB.

-

I appeared in a play the other evening. The audience got their money's worth - we gave them their money back when they left.

-

I used to steal art. I needed the Monet.

-

Pirates are great singers. They can hit the high Cs!

-

I went to a party at NASA. How do they organise it? They Planet.

-

What are Greek men called? Fhellas.

-

I went to the doctors and said I look like a pair of curtains. He told me to pull myself together.

-

What did the host of the strong alcoholic drinks conference say to open the event? Let the fun be gin.

-

I was burgled by some ants today - they were arrested for breaking and antering.

-

I wanted to join a committee for Spanish cars, but could not get a Seat on the table

-

 What is the punishment for bigamy in England? More than one mother in law.

-

I can't stand emojis. Words cannot express how much I hate them.

-

I always sleep in the nude. It's not that convenient on long haul flights.

-

I'm in a band called Cat's eyes - we play middle of

the road stuff.

-

I think my girlfriend is putting on weight. She fits in my wife's clothes.

-

My cat is training to be a doctor. He will be a medical kit.

-

What is the best thing to put in a pie? Teeth.

-

What is a fish with no eye called? Fsh.

-

I bought a huge crate of Tippex on the internet. What a big mistake.

-

What do cows use to buy things from? Cattlelogs.

-

What are alligator detectives called? Investigators.

-

My wife wants to leave me because I'm obsessed with rugby. I told her "let's have one more try".

-

I asked my American friend if he has his whole family for Thanksgiving dinner. He says he just has a turkey.

-

My friend replaced his bed with a trampoline, and didn't tell his wife. His wife hit the roof!

-

My watch is hungry. It went back four seconds.

-

I replaced my sandwich toaster but it does not work. I should have kept the old one - better the Breville you know.

-

I have a friend who wears a paper suit. His name is Russell.

-

What do skeletons order in a bar? A gin and tonic and a mop.

-

I worked at the candle factory. I got fired because I refused to work wick ends.

-

What do you get if you eat pi? Fat.

-

What is a boomerang that does not return called? A stick.

-

I asked my doctor to help me out. He said "what way did you come in?"

-

What is a rich elf called? Welfy.

-

I used to be conceited - now I'm perfect.

-

What can you see on small beaches? Micro waves.

-

What do cats climb in Nepal? A meowtain.

-

What is blue and smells like paint? Blue paint.

-

What do the Eiffel Tower and a tick have in common? They are paris-sites.

-

My farm is going well - it is growing.

-

My zombie friend came round to dinner the other day. He brought his ghoul friend.

-

I watched the weatherdog on TV. He says it is nippy outside.

-

My son asked me "can I have a book mark". Does he not know my name is Arthur?

-

I did jury today for someone accused of stealing doors. It was an open and shut case.

I find mountains funny - they are hillareas.

-

I still enjoy sex at 71. I live at 73.

-

How many lips are on a flower? Tulips.

-

I lost my luggage during a recent flight and sued the airline. I lost my case.

-

I have a tree that can fit in my hand - a palm tree.

-

What do you call a bear with no ear? B

-

What is a ghost's favourite drink? Ghoul-ade.

-

I read that humans eat more bananas than monkeys. Well I haven't eaten a monkey for ages.

-

Where did the egg farmer go on holiday? Monteneggro.

-

My son swallowed some coins. He is doing ok at the hospital - no change yet.

-

I was sitting in traffic for an hour today. In the end I was nearly run over.

-

My wife spent a fortune on perfume. She has no common scents.

-

I'm head of recruitment at my company. I avoid employing unlucky people by throwing half the job applications away.

-

I read in the paper how someone was tortured by having porridge poured over them. How gruel.

I let my ten year old son watch the TV after 10pm
- as long as he does not turn it on.

-

Where were the first French fried potatoes
cooked? In Greece.

-

My butcher introduced me to his wife. Meet Patty,
he said.

-

I know a manicurist and dentist who do not get
on. They are always fighting tooth and nail.

-

What is a fake noodle called? Impasta.

-

I worked in a timber factory and backed into a
wood sander. I got a little behind at work.

-

I'm a huge fan of renewable energy.

-

I'm looking forward to the new movie about constipation. it has not come out yet.

\-

What is a dog's favourite pizza? Puperoni.

\-

I'm a private detective. Last week I had to get a duck in to quack the case.

\-

I told a great joke about boxing yesterday. But nobody got the punchline.

\-

What do you call a thieving reptile? A crookigator.

\-

What vegetable is not served on a boat? Leek.

\-

My boss wished me a good day. So I went home.

\-

Which hand is it best to brush your teeth with. Neither - use a toothbrush.

I have an astronaut friend and told him a good way to stop his baby from crying. You rocket.

-

The cook at my restaurant did not fit in. He was in the wrong plaice and the wrong thyme.

-

I had a dream last night that I was making a salad. I was tossing and turning all night.

-

I don't trust left handed people. Something about them is not right.

-

What do you call a pig with three eyes? Piiig.

-

My doctor said I should have a protein shake at 11.30 every evening. But that is whey past my bedtime.

-

I used to work in a bank. But I gradually lost

interest.

-

My electrician is always watching the news channels. He likes to keep up with currant events.

-

Staircases are always up to something.

-

I could not work out where the sun came from. Then it dawned on me.

-

I swallowed a dictionary. Afterwards I had a thesaurus throat.

-

I went to a restaurant the other day and had the pelican. The bill was massive.

-

I asked my nurse girlfriend to marry me out side the hospital. She turned me down on medical grounds.

-

I'm writing a book on reverse psychology. I hope no one buys it.

-

Someone threw Omega 3 pills at me. Fortunately I only suffered super fish oil injuries.

-

My wife said she wanted either an iPhone or an iPad for her birthday. I bought her an iRon.

-

I was late for work yesterday and my boss said "you should have been here at 9 am." I said "what happened at 9 am?"

-

What is the difference between a pen and a pencil? Cil.

-

I was pleased to see my uncle left me a large house in his will. I'm not sure where Sod Hall is though.

-

I paid a bedmaker to make a king sized bed. but he has done a bunk.

My son was given a sofa and two armchairs. I have warned him about accepting suites from strangers.

-

What meows and is prickly. A catctus.

-

My local prosthetics shop is changing hands.

-

What uses up 20 parking spaces? 10 women drivers.

-

My wife said she is not concerned about rising fuel prices as she always puts £20 in.

-

I called my son Saturn. It has a ring to it.

-

I took six baskets to the supermarket yesterday as they say you should not put all your eggs in one basket.

I wanted to watch the Dracula movie on television - but the channel was encrypted.

-

What do you call someone with a shovel on their head? Doug.

-

I got a new laptop for the wife - it was a good trade.

-

Next week I'm entering a tight hat competition. I hope I can pull it off.

-

My wife does not understand me. She only speaks Welsh.

-

I wanted to take a course at college. I accidentally registered for the escapology course, but now i can't get out of it.

-

The banana went to the beach. He got sunburnt and in the end he was peeling.

-

What do bakers use to get to work? A piecycle.

-

I visited a ranch and the rancher said "can you help me round up 17 cows?" I said "it is 20 cows".

-

Balloons hate pop music.

-

I used to have an addiction to swimming. But I'm pleased to announce I have been dry for 5 years

-

Someone stole the soap from the bath. I think it was the robber ducky.

-

I'm selling my classical music shop. I'm glad to see the Bach of it.

-

I can't believe that I'm not allowed to wear the

shirt of my favourite sports team at work any more. I'm tempted to quit the funeral business.

-

I no longer have reindeer milk in my tea. I'm on a deery free diet.

-

My local bakery are not making shortbread any longer.

-

What is the name of the Cow communist leader? Chairman Moo.

-

What do birds use yo dry their dishes? The teat owl.

-

I came second in the World Anger Championships. I was outraged!

-

I watched a film about two oranges being rubbed together. It is called Pulp friction.

-

How do you hold a bat? By the handle.

-

My neighbour is a Satanist. Unfortunately he is dyslexic and sold his soul to Santa.

-

What sounds like a parrot and is coloured orange? A carrot.

-

Who is the patroon saint of topless dancers? St. Ripper.

-

I'm grateful to the student loan company for helping me at university. I don't think I can ever repay them

-

I keep thinking I'm a bell. I told my doctor and he told me to give him a ring if it happens again.

-

I find it hard to meet vegan women in nightclubs. They don't like cheesy lines.

What do Greek librarians have for lunch? Shh-kebabs.

-

I have started a career as a photographer. It is developing well.

-

My friend said to me "cheer up, you could be stuck in a hole full of water". I know he means well.

-

The head of Ikea has taken over as Prime Minister. He is assembling his team.

-

 I went to the doctor as I had spots on my back. The doctor said "don't worry - they are benign". I said " I though there were 10".

-

Some say stealing is wrong. I don't buy it.

-

I went to the emergency ward the other day and said I'd hurt my arm in several places. The doctor said "don't go there then".

-

I phoned my Fish and chip shop yesterday and asked if they do takeaway. "Yes" they replied. I said "what is 89-67."

-

What is blue black and white? A zebra who is depressed.

-

I gave my friend some eggs, flour, butter and a whisk for his birthday. It's an Ikea birthday cake.

-

I'm surprised to hear you cannot make the sound of a coconut by banging two sides of a horse together.

-

I had a Hawaiian pizza for dinner yesterday, but i burn it. I should have put the oven on aloha temperature.

-

In the last few years I have been addicted to soap. But thankfully I'm clean now.

-

I was bitten by a vampire in Iceland last winter. I got frost-bite.

-

There is a ghost that haunts the piece of road near my house. It's a dead end.

-

My wife thinks I'm the salt of the earth. As a result she keeps me in the cellar.

-

How do you drown a hipster. Put him in the mainstream.

-

What do people at space rocket sites eat? Launching meat.

-

I use Beefstew as my password on my computer. But I'm not sure it is stroganoff.

-

I gave a donation to the campaign for a new swimming pool today. I gave a glass of water.

-

I tried to join Paranoids Anonymous. But I don't think they wanted me as a member.

-

My doctor said a banana a day keeps the colon clean. I wish he had told me you have to eat them!

-

I went into a shop to buy a packet of helicopter crisps. They did not have any so I had plain.

-

Police are using lots of resources searching for a robber who is stealing blunt pencils. what's the point?

-

A red ship crashed into a blue ship last week. The two crews were marooned.

-

I sent my hearing aid to be repaired three weeks ago but have not heard anything since.

-

 Scientists have crossed a cow and a smurf to create blue cheese.

-

What is small and hairy and sounds like a horse? A coconut cut in half.

-

I'm sure I've had that mustard before. It is Dijon vu.

-

I'm in a dispute over a pie company about a defective steak and kidney pudding. I decided to suet.

-

I was sceptical about having a vaccine, but in the end I gave it a shot.

-

Arthur Baker invented the door knocker. He won the Nobel prize.

I'm a television repairman. I got married last week. The reception was wonderful.

-

Shopping centres? Once you've seen one you've seen the mall.

-

My local newspaper visits the ice cream parlour for stories. They are looking for a scoop.

-

I'm reading a fantastic book about anti-gravity. It's simply impossible to put down.

-

I entered a pun contest, sending in 10 puns. But no pun in ten did.

-

I am a man of culture - I eat Greek yogurt every morning.

-

I'd like to bring back the name Lance. In

Mediaeval times people were called Lance a lot.

-

I went to London Zoo and there was a French baguette in a cage. The zoo keeper said it was bread in captivity.

-

Who shaves 25 times a day? A barber.

-

I'm helping monkeys with depression. I'm always there when the chimps are down.

-

I saw an advert for a tv today which said "TV for sale £10 - volume is stuck on the highest setting". i though I can't turn that down.

-

I like puzzle games such as crosswords and sudoku. I even like jigsaws. I do not like dot to dot - you have to draw the line somewhere.

-

I'm not going to have a brain transplant, but i may change my mind.

I going to the vegan club to meet a girl I've never met herbivore.

-

I have a helpful skeleton friend. he always lends a hand.

-

I wanted to train as an auctioneer. But I was put off as you have to know lots.

-

Two fish are in a tank. One of the fish says "how do you drive this?"

-

I visited the library to ask about a certain book about turtles. "hardback?" said the librarian. "Yes" I replied "with little legs and heads.

-

I put in a few extra hours at work. I work in a clock factory.

-

A large batch of suntan lotion has shown to be

faulty. That is going to cause a lot of red faces.

-

A container ship sunk the other day. I went to see what was washed up and saw microwaves.

-

I have a young elf who lives next door. He is doing his gnome work now.

-

How can I make Easter easier? Replace the t with an i.

-

Dogs are not great dancer as they have two left feet.

-

My pet rabbit runs a jewellers. He has 14 carrot rings in it.

-

In King Arthur's court the best gift giver was Sir Prize.

-

What is a maybe? A bee that can't make up its mind.

-

Thieves were caught robbing a bakery. They were caught bread handed.

-

My pony was giving a speech yesterday. He had to have a glass of water as he was a little horse.

-

What happens to chemists when they die? They barium.

-

I'm trying to invent an insect repellent, but I'm starting from scratch.

-

My self defence class is exhausting. All that running.

-

I cool my hot drink before drinking - it is safe tea first.

-

A man stole my diary, and I have just heard he has died. My thoughts are with his family.

\-

I'm a teacher and I always test the water when I go to the beach.

\-

It rained cats and dogs last week. I stepped in a poodle.

\-

Three years ago my doctor told me i was going deaf. I have not heard from him since.

\-

I have a phobia of buildings - it is a complex complex.

\-

What causes dry skin? A towel.

\-

What do people in Greenland eat in their salad? Iceberg lettuce.

\-

Why was the mathematics book unhappy?
Because of all of its problems.

-

What flies and has four wheels? A waste disposal
truck.

-

I'm really awful at curling. But there is broom for
improvement.

-

How do I describe the world's worst thesaurus? It
is awful and awful.

-

 Where do sheep go to get their haircut? The
Baabaa shop.

-

Why did the golfer have two pairs of trousers? In
case he got a hole in one.

-

People in France do not like fast food - they eat
snails.

-

My wife is so childish - she sank my boats in my bath.

-

Why is a sports stadium always cool? Because it is full of fans.

-

I went to Alaska to search for gold, but it did not pan out.

-

I made a bicycle from spaghetti. My wife did not believe it would work but changed her mind when I rode pasta.

-

I meditate often. It is better than sitting around and doing nothing.

-

Dracula and Frankenstein have opened up a pancake shop. The place gives me the crepes.

-

I have lots of horses living in my

neighhhhbourhood.

-

When I play golf i take an extra pair of socks. In
case I get a hole in one.

-

Is it worth writing with a broken pen? No it is
pointless.

-

I'm not sure why puns about trees are not more
poplar.

-

I swallowed some daffodil bulbs. Doctors say they
should be out in the spring.

-

I'm thinking of become a mind reader. Do you
have any thoughts?

-

What marital arts do vegetable study? Carotte.

-

I was going to give a urine sample yesterday. but

I lost my bottle.

-

I was a member of an elite secret gourmet
society. I spilled the beans.

-

I had a garage sale yesterday. I gave away my
dead batteries free of charge.

-

I baked some special German Christmas bread.
But it was Stollen.

-

What does a dyslexic Yorkshireman wear on his
head? A cat flap.

-

What do you call a Greek prisoner. Concrete.

-

I watch the chicken 1500 metres at the Olympics.
Poultry in motion.

-

Apple has announced the iKnife. It is cutting edge

technology.

-

I had salsa poured over me. I was covered from my head tomatoe.

-

I used to date a whisky maker - I love her still.

-

Fairy stories are wonderful, although sometimes they do dragon.

-

What do you call a magician who has lost his magic? Ian.

-

Why do birds fly to warmer places in the winter? It is easier than walking.

-

Which hand do people write better with? none of them - a pen is better.

-

Construction workers were digging at the local

church - it is holely ground.

-

What is an Estonian's favourite curry? Balti.

-

What do you call a sarcastic bear? A panduh.

-

A man walked into a bar. And broke his nose.

-

Why was the mushroom popular at parties? Because he is a fungi.

-

Where do monkeys do outdoor cooking? On the gorilla.

-

What is 500 miles long and purple? The grape wall of China.

-

What do you call an angry insect? A croissant.

-

There was a kidnapping at my local school - but he woke up.

-

Why do fish live in salt water? They do not like pepper as it makes then sneeze.

-

I went to a party last night. I was hoping to take some leftovers but my plans were foiled.

-

My music shop was robbed last week. The burglars got away with the lute.

-

I just burned off 2500 calories - I left my cake in the oven too long.

-

What do you call a Judge with no fingers? Justice Thumbs.

-

Police arrested the world champion tongue twister speaker. He is going to get a tough sentence.

My wife rang to say the Windows had frozen. I said she should pour over hot water. Later she rang back to say the computer was not working.

-

I put an ad in the local paper saying "wife wanted". I received numerous replies. They were all from men saying "you can have mine".

-

You can't trust the King of the Jungle. He is often lion.

-

Does anyone know how to correct plastic surgery that has gone wrong. If so I am all ears.

-

I sent my friends who have moved house a set of radiators as a house warming present.

-

What dog does magic tricks? Labracadabrador

-

A book fell on my head today. I blame myshelf.

-

I had roast parrot for dinner yesterday. It is repeating on me now.

-

My neighbour his me with a number of string instruments; he does have a history of violins.

-

What has five fingers, but is not your hand? someone else's hand.

-

I took my teddy bear out for dinner last night. He was stuffed at the end of the meal.

-

My wife likes really expensive coffee. It costa fortune.

-

 What do snails use to talk to each other? Shell phones.

-

My vacuum cleaner is for sale. It was just

collecting dust in my house.

-

Saturday and Sunday are the strongest days. The other days are weekdays.

-

I heard strange rumours about butter. I don't spread them though.

-

A tiger escaped from the zoo yesterday. Upon hearing the news I puma pants.

-

I have a crystal growing out of my thumb. It is a qwart.

-

What did the frog order in the restaurant? French flies.

-

Why did the Welshman's fridge drip water? It had leeks in it.

-

What does a clock do if it hungry after dinner? It goes back four seconds.

-

The cinema tried to stop me smuggling chocolate into the cinema. But I have a few Twix up my sleeve.

-

What did the drummer call his four daughters? Anna 1 Anna 2 Anna 4 Anna 4

-

Can I describe myself in one word? "not very good at following instructions".

-

What is the difference between a mother in law and an outlaw? The outlaw is wanted.

-

I've started an engraving course. We have not scratched the surface yet.

-

I don't think Mona Lisa was that attractive. She was no oil painting.

The roadsweeper was late for work - he overslept.

-

I want to put glue on my set of antique pistols. I was advised against it but I'm sticking to my guns.

-

What do you get if you cross Tom Cruise and a climate change conference. Emission Impossible.

-

I threw some butter out the window yesterday. I wanted to see a butterfly.

-

I told my wife that I find black underwear sexy so she stopped washing mine.

-

I paid £30 for an Oxo cube yesterday. The stock market has gone mad.

-

I poured cement on a burglar, and created a hardened criminal.

What do witches eat on holiday? A sand-witch.

-

An Apple shop has been robbed. Police are looking for iWitnesses.

-

How does the sea say hello to someone? It waves.

-

Shakespeare is banned from the pubs in my town. He's bard.

-

I did a walking tour of the Nordic area. I was glad to get to the Finnish.

-

What does a vampire doctor say to the patients in his waiting room? Necks please.

-

What happens to the Queen's old clothes? They get throne away.

-

What do dinosaurs look for at the bottom of the ocean? T-wrecks.

-

I went to see my wife in hospital and took her flowers. My girlfriend loved them.

-

The world origami championships are on television this evening. On paperview.

-

The television weatherman reacted angrily after being criticised for his cold weather forecasts. He said from now on it is no more mist an ice guy.

-

The picture was sentenced to ten years in prison. It was framed.

-

I bought Darth Vader some gifts for Christmas. But he knew what they were as he felt my presence.

-

My wife called me lazy in the supermarket. I was so shocked I fell out of the shopping trolly.

\-

I have a new garden that needs plants. But I have not botany yet.

\-

I love the rotation of the Earth. It makes my day.

\-

I suffer from kleptomania. I take something for it.

\-

I'm selling broken puppets - no strings attached.

\-

I went to the doctor as I have an illness where I keep making jobs about airports. The doctor says it is terminal.

\-

I'm selling my DeLorean because I only drive it from time to time.

\-

How does Father Christmas wash his hands? With

hand sanitizer.

-

Fruits and vegetables make me feel so good - from my head tomatoes.

-

I'm trying to build up a collection of my favourite works by European composers. I've nearly completed my Liszt?

-

I was cleaning up the local park as part of a volunteer gardening groups. Aliens landed and said "take me to your weeder."

-

I wanted to borrow a book on bigfoot from the library. The librarian said it was in the large print section.

-

Count Dracula is remodelling his castle and moving the furniture around. He is doing some Fang-shui.

-

What is an old snowman called? Walter.

I turned up at John McEnroe's fancy dress party dressed as Harry Potter's grandfather. He said "you cannot be Sirius".

-

I went to see an overweight psychic medium to see what it in store for my future. He was a four chin teller.

-

I'm trying to get a job compiling the Oxford English dictionary. I asked a friend to put in a word for me.

-

I have finally discovered a joke about herbs. It's about thyme!

-

A funeral was held today for Britain's unfunniest man. His best joke was read out to a minutes silence.

-

My neighbour was washing his car with his on yesterday. I don't know why he does not just use a sponge.

-

The witch had to go to the doctor as she was suffering from dizzy spells.

-

I had a job at an orange juice factory but got fired. I could not concentrate.

-

Why do people put birthday candles on the top of a cake? You cannot put them on the bottom.

-

How many apples grow on an average tree? All of them.

-

I bought some shares yesterday as I was lonely. It is nice to have a bit of company.

-

Cher has a twin. They formed a music group called Cher and Cher alike.

-

I run a sweet shop and I had to discuss the finances with the bank manager. We had a candied conversation.

-

Two dyslexics walked into a bra.........

-

A cement mixer and prison van crashed into each other. Police are looking for 20 hardened criminals.

-

I was injured last week in a peek a boo accident. I was in ICU.

-

The rain is depressing my wife - she is just staring through the window. I should really let her in.

-

I'd like to thank my neighbour who explained the word many to me. It really means a lot.

-

My friend works at the chocolate factory. A shelf containing boxes of chocolate bar fell on him and he was trapped underneath them. He shouted for help saying "the milky bars are on me". But everyone just cheered.

-

Someone stole my trainers. I would like to say to the thief: "you can run but you can't hide".

-

My mate said an onion is the only food that can make you cry. so I threw a coconut at his head.

-

An Englishman, an Italian, a Russian, two Swedes, a Zimbabwean, a Czech, 3 Spaniards, a Pole, 2 Frenchmen, an Australian and 2 Vietnamese went to a restaurant. The waiter said to the group "sorry you can't come in - no Thai."

-

I thought I was good in bed. Then i discovered my girlfriends had asthma.

-

What do you call an accident prone bird? An owl.

-

Someone knocked on the door this morning. It

was a 5 ft beetle and it punched me in the face. There is a nasty bug going around.

-

My friend Marge has been ill for a long time. I can't believe she's not better.

-

I love boiled eggs in the morning. They are hard to beat.

-

I was trying to work out why a ball get getting bigger and bigger. Then it hit me.

-

I mixed up the word Yazuka and Jacuzzi. I'm now in hot water with the Japanese mafia.

-

A glass of water does not know the whole of the alphabet - only H to O.

-

It has been announced that Holy water can be made by putting water in a pot and boiling the hell out of it.

-

My credit card was stolen last month. It is not too bad as the thief is spending less money than my wife did.

-

I got some blackberries stuck down my throat. I nearly choked on my own Vimto.

-

My neighbour is an electrician and did some work on my house. I was shocked how bad he was.

-

Why are the pyramids in Egypt? The are too heavy to move somewhere else.

-

My friend was burning her credit card statements the other day. Her name is Bernadette.

-

There was a storm last night which hit my farm. I'm not sure if my barn is damaged - I have not found it yet.

-

There is a strike at the potato farm. It will lead to a chip shortage

-

Someone stole my supplies of Red Bull energy drink. How do they sleep at night?

-

I always shout cauliflower and broccoli. I may have florets disease.

-

I managed to get an invite to the funeral directors dinner. The organiser said "the morgue the merrier".

-

A man washed the car with his son. Why did he not use a cloth?

-

A friend at work had his last day yesterday. We bought him a comb as a parting gift.

-

I work in a bank. A woman came in today with two £50 notes in her ears. Her account was £100 in arrears.

-

I bought my youngest son a new lamp. You should have seen his face light up when he received it!

-

I'm reading a book about Stockholm Syndrome. I did not like it at first, but I'm really enjoying it now.

-

I was watching that TV show about a motorway maintenance team in a medieval fantasy world. It's called Game of Cones.

-

What do you call a Scotsman with flatulence? Bravefart.

-

My neighbour was playing a Lionel Ritchie song last night. It was annoying as it was all night long.

-

My vegan friends are now in a relationship. It was love at first soy-t.

-

I used to run a successful origami business. But unfortunately it folded.

-

I took a photo of Michael J. Fox at the garden centre yesterday. He had his back to the fuchsias

-

I know people think it is risky for me to drink break fluid - but I can stop any time I want to.

-

Did you hear that I have been invited to join a new Suspense Club? The first rule is......

-

I watched a riveting documentary yesterday - on how ships are held together.

-

What do you call a man wearing a raincoat in a cemetery? Max Bygraves.

-

My wife struggles with cooking - she uses the smoke alarm as a timer.

-

I bought an ancient rock statue from Ireland yesterday. But on the bottom it had the Made in China logo. Obviously a sham rock.

-

What swings through the jungle and is yellow? Tarzipan.

-

I'm friends with 25 letters in the alphabet. I don't know why.

-

My financial advisor asked me to invest in Bonds. I bought a blue-ray box set of the movies.

-

My dog ate my dictionary and I had to rescue it from him. I took the words right out of his mouth.

-

It is easy to win over a fat person - piece of cake.

-

What do you get if you cross a car with Quasimodo. The hatchback of Notre Dam.

-

I knew someone who laundered money through a tennis club. It was a good racket.

-

It is diarrhoea awareness week this week - it runs until Friday.

-

I own a bakery and a restaurant for cannibals. I have my fingers in several pies.

-

I know a veterinarian with a sore throat. He is a hoarse doctor.

-

What do you get if you cross a pop singer with a plastic inflatable object? A Beyonce castle.

-

Last week I knocked on a door, crossed the road, walked into a bar and changed a lightbulb. My life is a joke.

-

I held a business meeting at a campsite. It was an in tents discussion.

-

A man with two left feet went to the seaside. He took along his flip-flips.

-

I went to the toy store to look for Arnold Schwarzenegger toys. i asked where they were and the assistant said "Aisle B, back."

-

I told my doctor I would be doing the stitches on my leg myself. He said suture self.

-

I can't eat Lebanese food. I'm always falafel afterwards.

-

What do nuclear physicists eat? Fission chips.

-

What do you get if you cross a sheep with a kangaroo? A woollen jumper.

-

I'm half way through reading a horror story in Braille. Something horrible is going to happen - I can feel it!

-

Why are skeletons afraid of things? They don't have any guts.

-

My French neighbour always wears sandals. His name is Philippe Philoppe.

-

I ate a cake shaped like a clock yesterday. It was delicious - I went back for seconds.

-

I'd admire these Olympic athletes for all the hard work they put in. They should give them a medal.

-

If all T's were silent, we would never hear the end of it.

-

Crabs do not give any money to charity as they are shellfish.

Autocorrect is awful I hope the creator burns in Hello.

-

Polar bears are voting in their election - in the north poll.

-

I used to work with some vampires. They were a real pain in the neck.

-

The hospital rang me up and said my wife is critical. I said "I know!".

-

Where was the McDonald's burger invented? Macau.

-

What is an electricians favourite sweet? Shockalote.

-

What do rabbits use to go on holiday? An

hareplane.

-

I went into the library yesterday and said to the librarian "big mac and fries please". She said "this is a library". I whispered "big mac and fries please".

-

The fact that the Earth is rotating really makes my day.

-

I decided to change all my passwords to "kenny". I now have kenny log ons.

-

A CNN correspondent was involved in a mustard gas attack during a war, and a pepper spray attack reporting on a demonstration. He is now a seasoned reporter.

-

I've just come back from a once in a lifetime holiday. Never again!

-

Where do bees go on holiday? Pollenesia.

My wife asked me to clear the table. I did so after a run up.

-

If I received 50p for every maths exam I failed. I'd have £7.20 now.

-

Do I believe in reincarnation? I prefer milk.

-

I sent a letter to a trout yesterday. I dropped him a line.

-

I have been asked by my doctor to only eat 1700 calories a day. I'm not sure how many I'm allowed to eat at night.

-

My wife has one leg shorter than the other. Her name is Eileen.

-

I bought Spiderman pyjamas today. I do hope he

likes them.

-

I lost my job at the theatre as a set designer. I left without making a scene.

-

I like to take a dip in the pool - hummus.

-

Which jungle dwelling animal is the stupidest? A polar bear.

-

I ate too much food at Halloween. I had autumyache.

-

The man who invented the windowsill is a ledg-end.

-

My archaeology office blew up. It is in ruins now.

-

My coffee taste like dirt even though it was ground this morning.

-

What English word is always spelt incorrectly?
Incorrectly.

-

I grew up in a poor part of town in Italy - a
spaghetto.

-

What is a snails' favourite citrus fruit? Slime.

-

I married Miss Right. Unfortunately her first name
is always.

-

The hospital told me I had type A blood. But they
made a mistake - it was type-o.

-

Napoleon helped design a wonderful range of
clothes. He always had a hand in them

-

I waited for the Irish ice cream van yesterday, but
it had melted.

What is a man with a rubber toe called? Roberto.

-

My dog stopped the music on my media player.
He pawsed it

-

I have some vegetables who are humanitarians.
They want world peas.

-

I have a phobia of stairs and escalators. I take
steps to avoid them.

-

This joke book is great for the environment -
100% of the jokes are recycled.

-

Dr: This patient is dying. What blood type does he
have"?

-

What is faster, cold or hot? Hot as you can catch a
cold.

Where can you find more letters than the
alphabet? A post office.

-

What is the nicest vegetable? The sweet potato.

-

I had a dream about a man in metal suit chasing
after me. It was a knightmare.

-

A city in Yorkshire has gone missing. Police are
looking for Leeds.

-

I have invented the strongest acid known to man.
But I can't find a container for it.

-

Whiteboards are a remarkable invention.

-

I ate too much bread yesterday. I had to go to the
doctor as I was feeling crummy.

-

What is Dracula's favourite ice cream flavour?
Veinilla.

-

What do firefighters eat with their cheese?
Firecrackers.

-

My green grocer is going on holiday next week -
to Pear-is.

-

I took my banana to hospital yesterday. It was
not peeling well.

-

I told a great joke about chemistry the other day.
But here was no reaction.

-

I went to the fresh fish counter in the
supermarket today. He said he had counted 13
fish.

-

I was robbed by six dwarves the other evening -

not happy.

-

Frank Sinatra when asked if he had eaten many sandwiches in his life said: "baguettes, I had a few, but then again too few to mention".

-

I had a job making keyboards, but I was fired. I was not putting enough shifts in.

-

I received a telephone call today. The caller sneezed and hung up. I hate cold calls.

-

A man could not pay for his exorcism - he was repossessed.

-

I lost my apples and searched for them, but did not find them. It was a fruit less search.

-

What is a mummy's favourite music? Wrap music.

-

What salad do they eat in space? Rocket.

-

I'm not looking for a career. Just the payments.

-

I won dentist of the year last year. I got a little plaque.

-

I always eat with my dog - I like ruffage with my meal

-

How can you make an artichoke? By strangling it.

-

Nurse: B Positive

Dr: Ok. He is going to pull through!

-

What car is cheap enough to buy? A Ford

-

What is a golfers favourite pudding? Parfait.

-

I saw a tomato blush yesterday. It spotted a salad dressing.

-

Archaeologists cannot find the location to the pharaoh's tomb. The location is encrypted.

-

I made an octopus laugh last week - with ten tickles.

-

I left a £20 in my jeans and washed them Police have charged me with money laundering.

-

My bank password has been hacked again. Looks like the cat will get another new name.

-

I told my wife that she draws her eyebrows on too high. She looked surprised.

-

I always make sure and knock on the fridge before opening. Just in case there is a salad dressing.

-

I had a children's meal at McDonalds today. His mother was absolutely furious.

-

I've got a story about my snooker cue attachments. Do you want to hear the rest?

-

If you cannot spell Armageddon, don't worry, it is not the end of the world.

-

I keep thinking I'm a burglar. I'll have to take something for it.

-

Someone said I should buy coffin. That is the last thing I'll need.

-

I added insult to injury yesterday - I signed a rude greeting on my friends cast on his broken leg.

-

What are 3.1% of sailors? Pi-rates.

-

Why did the King have a long face? Because he was a ruler.

-

A man was shot with a starter pistol It is believed to be race related.

-

Some people knocked on my door yesterday wanting to sell me a vacuum cleaner and talk about god. They were Je-hoovers witnesses.

-

One of my children asked me what an eclipse was. I said "no son".

-

Which Star Wars character works in a clothes shop? Mannequin Skywalker.

-

What is slippery and a foot long. A slipper.

-

I tried to push the envelope, but it was still stationary.

-

I don't know what the word Armageddon, but it is not the end of the world.

-

If you had six oranges and a melon on one hand, and four pears and a pineapple on another hand, what would you have? Very big hands.

-

Historians are not sure what pencil Shakespeare used - 2B or not 2B.

-

How do you make a pie go to sleep? Sing a lullapie.

-

I got a new remote control for all my media in the house. It has changed everything!

-

I had a business building stairs. Business was up and down.

-

It is easy to talk to giants. Just use big words.

-

Definition of being working class? A TV bigger than the bookcase.

-